CONTENTS

MISSION IMPROBABLE

Welcome! I'm glad you could come. Who am I? I am the Mystery Master and I'm here to solve mysteries and explore the unexplained. You can help me in trying to separate fact from fiction.

I've got a real historical puzzle for you. To find the answer to this one, you'll have to go back at least 1,500 years to search for one of history's greatest legends. King Arthur is thought to be a brave ruler of Britain during the Dark Ages. The story of his victories and the adventures of his knights and the wizard Merlin have been retold by many writers and storytellers over the centuries.

3800 16 0040716 1

High Life Highland

Did KING ARTHUR Exist?

Nick Hunter

raintree

a Capstone company —

HIGH LIFE HIGHLAND	HIGHLAND LIBRARIES
3800 16 0040716 1	
Askews & Holts	Mar-2017
942.014	£8.99
WITHDRAWN	

Raintree is an imprint of Capstone Global Library Limited, a company incorporated in England and Wales having its registered office at 264 Banbury Road, Oxford, OX2 7DY – Registered company number: 6695582

www.raintree.co.uk
myorders@raintree.co.uk

Text © Capstone Global Library Limited 2016
The moral rights of the proprietor have been asserted.

All rights reserved. No part of this publication may be reproduced in any form or by any means (including photocopying or storing it in any medium by electronic means and whether or not transiently or incidentally to some other use of this publication) without the written permission of the copyright owner, except in accordance with the provisions of the Copyright, Designs and Patents Act 1988 or under the terms of a licence issued by the Copyright Licensing Agency, Saffron House, 6–10 Kirby Street, London EC1N 8TS (www.cla.co.uk). Applications for the copyright owner's written permission should be addressed to the publisher.

Edited by James Benefield and Helen Cox Cannons
Designed by Steve Mead
Original illustrations © Capstone Global Library Limited
Picture research by Kelly Garvin
Production by Victoria Fitzgerald
Originated by Capstone Global Library Limited 2015
Printed and bound in China

ISBN 978 1 4747 1475 4 (hardback)
19 18 17 16 15
10 9 8 7 6 5 4 3 2 1

ISBN 978 1 4747 1493 8 (paperback)
20 19 18 17 16
10 9 8 7 6 5 4 3 2 1

British Library Cataloguing in Publication Data
A full catalogue record for this book is available from the British Library.

Acknowledgements
Alamy: Hilary Morgan, 11, Lifestyle pictures, 33 (top right); Corbis: Bettmann, 39 (middle), Skyscan, 8 (bottom), 22 (b), University of Leicester, 38 (b); Getty Images: DeAgostini, 30 (middle right), Fine Art Images/Heritage Images, 14 (tr), Geography Photos.UIG, 24 (b), GraphicaArtis, 10 (bottom right), Heritage Images, 12 (b), Leon Neal, 27 (bottom left), Oli Scarff, 9 (tr), Print Collector, 25 (b), 29 (br), Time Life Pictures, 26, Universal History Archive/UIG, 13 (mr); Newscom/Eddie Keogh/Rueters, 6 (m); Mary Evans Picture Library, 34 (b), Frank Furness, 41 (mr); Newscom/REX, 36 (b); North Wind Picture Archive, 16 (middle left); Shutterstock: Adrian Zenz, 38-39 (background), Aleksandar Mijatovic, 20-21 (top background), Anki Hoglund, 15 (background), Anne Greenwood, 11 (background), Artindo, 19 (b), bazzier, 24 (tr), BigganVi 6-7 (background), buchan, 12 (top left), Cattallina, 8-9 (background), daseugen, 40 (background), Dmitry Naumov, 15 (b), Dolimac, 22-23 (background), Ensuper, 18-19 (background), Esteban De Armas, 16-17 (background), Fer Gregory, 10 (background), FXQuadro, 27(right), Fulcanelli, 32 (b), Gavin Morrison, 5 (b), GlebStock, 33 (background), Ian McDonald, 35 (m), Justin Black, 20 (b), kevin bampton, 31 (b), Masson, cover, Mateusz Pohl, 37-36 (background), Matthew Collingwood, 32 (background), nikkytok, 7 (b), Patalakha Serg, 24-25 (background), Patrick Wang, 17 (m), Petrafler, 25 (tr), Sergey Nivens, 30-31 (background), Targn Pleiades, 12-13 (background), Tischenko Irina, 41 (background), Unholy Vault Designs, 28-29 (background), Vertyr, 20-21 (bottom background), 21 (b), ZRyzner, 32 (background); Superstock: Rob Taylor/Loop Images, 21 (tl), Travel Pix Collection/Jon Arnold Images, 19 (top); The Image Works: Newagen Archive, 28 (m)

Artistic elements: Shutterstock: agsandrew, Bruce Rolff, Eky Studio, Maksim Kabakou, Nik Merkulov.

Every effort has been made to contact copyright holders of material reproduced in this book. Any omissions will be rectified in subsequent printings if notice is given to the publisher.

All the internet addresses (URLs) given in this book were valid at the time of going to press. However, due to the dynamic nature of the internet, some addresses may have changed, or sites may have changed or ceased to exist since publication. While the author and publisher regret any inconvenience this may cause readers, no responsibility for any such changes can be accepted by either the author or the publisher.

The legend of King Arthur

A famous mention of Arthur comes from Nennius's book called *History of the Britons*, written in 830 CE:

"Then Arthur, with the kings of Britain, fought against [the Saxons] in those days, but Arthur himself was dux bellorum [commander] in these battles."

INVESTIGATION TIPS

WARNING!
Remember, not all the evidence you'll find is reliable. The writer Nennius wrote the first history of King Arthur around 300 years after the time of the king. As well as written documents that may be telling the truth, we need to pay attention to evidence from under the ground, dug up by archaeologists.

Nennius also lists 12 great victories, including the Battle of Badon Hill "in which there fell in one day 960 men from one charge of Arthur, and no one struck them down except Arthur himself, and in all the war he emerged as victor."

Sounds like a tough guy, doesn't he? There's just one catch. We don't know if King Arthur ever existed at all. Your mission is to use all the available evidence to try to solve this mystery once and for all: Did King Arthur really exist?

The legends say that King Arthur was buried in the ancient town of Glastonbury in Somerset.

How to be a history detective

If you want to find out what happened in the past, you have to dig – not just in the ground, but also through old books and documents. Any mention of King Arthur could give us the vital clue we need to solve this mystery.

This collection of Anglo–Saxon treasures dates from shortly after the time when Arthur may have lived. It was found buried in a field in England.

THE SCIENCE

What do archaeologists do?

Archaeologists study physical objects and evidence to find the truth, just like detectives. Archaeologists dig up historical sites to find clues, such as weapons, coins or pieces of pottery. They can find out when these items were made, what they are made from and other details that tell us about the people who created and used them.

If we were looking at a recent historical mystery, we could look at photos or films for evidence. Perhaps we could even talk to eyewitnesses who saw what happened. When you are looking at things that happened 1,500 years ago, those clues are not available. You need to study ancient sites and remains to create a picture of the past.

Written evidence

We have to be careful which books and documents we trust, especially if we don't know much about the writer. Sometimes writers in history want to promote a particular point of view. Some writers might be trying to please a king or queen. Others might be writing many years after the events they're describing.

INVESTIGATION TIPS

Detective equipment

If you want to search for the truth about King Arthur, there are some tools that would be useful. For example:

- Warm and waterproof clothes: The secrets of King Arthur's life are not hidden in some dusty desert or steaming jungle but in Britain. If you go out to explore, keep warm and dry!

- A metal detector and a spade: Metal detectors can help you locate priceless hidden clues, and you'll need a spade to dig them up.

- A library card: You'll have to investigate some ancient handwritten documents, often in other languages such as Latin or French.

Make sure you get permission to use a metal detector on somebody's land.

THE LEGEND OF KING ARTHUR

Before you start to look at the evidence about the real Arthur, we need to explore background details. There are legends about the "once and future king" that have grown over hundreds of years. From those, we can start to separate fact from fiction.

Defender of Britain

By the 5th century CE, the Romans had ruled much of southern Britain for 400 years. But their empire was crumbling. Around the year 410, the legions of the Roman army left Britain to help defend Ancient Rome from invaders. At the same time, the coast of Britain was being raided by Anglo-Saxon invaders from what is now called Germany.

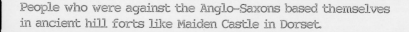

People who were against the Anglo-Saxons based themselves in ancient hill forts like Maiden Castle in Dorset.

Around the 440s, more and more Anglo-Saxons began to settle in southern England. They clashed with the native British population, mainly made up of a mix of Celts and Romans. The Britons fought back. According to legend, their leader was a chieftain called Arthur.

Twelve battles

The chieftain Arthur is said to have led his British forces in 12 battles against the invaders. This finally gave him a great victory at the Battle of Badon Hill. All these events may be true, but the details were only written down by Nennius almost 300 years later. Sometimes it's not always easy to separate historical facts from fiction.

This helmet belonged to an Anglo-Saxon king.

INVESTIGATION TIPS

The Dark Ages

The time when Arthur is said to have fought the Anglo-Saxons was the start of a time called the Dark Ages in Britain. The Dark Ages are so called because we know so little about what happened during this period. There are few reliable written records of the time, which might have told us about Arthur. This makes your job as a history detective even more difficult.

ONCE AND FUTURE KING

The legend of Arthur grew over the centuries. In popular stories, he became more than just a Celtic chieftain who battled the Anglo-Saxons. The legend we know today was created by medieval writers from the 12th century onwards.

In this legend, Arthur the warrior becomes the lost son of King Uther Pendragon, born at Tintagel, Cornwall. At the age of 15, Arthur pulled a sacred sword from a stone and was crowned king. Arthur ruled Britain from his castle at Camelot, alongside Queen Guinevere, the brave Knights of the Round Table and the magician Merlin.

According to legend, Arthur had to fight to become king after he pulled the sacred sword from the stone.

Things do not end well. Arthur discovers that Guinevere has fallen in love with his bravest knight, Lancelot. Arthur faces a challenge for the throne from Mordred (in some versions of the legend, this is his son). Finally, Arthur is fatally injured at the Battle of Camlann.

Holy Grail

Versions of this legend were originally written down during the great age of knights and castles. This might explain why it is full of heroic knights. Arthur's story was also mixed up with other legends, such as the quest to find the Holy Grail (see pages 16 and 17). The Grail was believed to be the cup that Jesus Christ drank from at the Last Supper, according to Christian beliefs.

Over the centuries that followed, many books and then films have changed the legend of Arthur. It is now a long way from the first stories of a Celtic warrior. Your job is to try to unravel the facts from the legends.

As the legends grew, Arthur and his warriors were thought of as medieval knights.

TOP SECRET

The first mentions of Arthur may come from ancient Welsh stories. *The Mabinogion* is a collection of tales that were translated in the 1800s. No one can be sure quite how ancient these tales are, but they include several stories of Arthur's court.

THE EVIDENCE:
Birth of a legend

To find the real identity of the legendary King Arthur, we need to get away from stories of knights and castles and back to basics. We have not found evidence left by Arthur, so where else can we look?

Aside from *The Mabinogion*, our first known account is from Nennius. His *History of the Britons*, written in about 830 CE, is probably the first mention of Arthur in writing. It's a good place to start, but there are problems. Nennius did not know Arthur: in fact, he was writing nearly 300 years after the events he wrote about. He was hardly an eyewitness to these great battles. Can anyone else help us to pin down the real Arthur?

This handwritten manuscript of Nennius's *History of the Britons* is one of the key clues to the truth about Arthur.

The monk Gildas wrote his own history of Britain around the time that Arthur might have lived. He tells the story of Britain in ruins and Britons fighting back against the Anglo-Saxon invaders. Gildas never mentions Arthur, but he does mention the Battle of Badon Hill. This was where Nennius claimed that Arthur won a great victory. In Gildas's story, the leader of the Britons is called Ambrosius, a noble Roman. Was Ambrosius linked to Arthur in some way?

TOP SECRET

In the 5th century, after the end of Roman rule, different chieftains and tribal leaders ruled different parts of Britain. We know the names of some of the chieftains, such as Vortigern (see picture below) who ruled in the southeast. But was Arthur one of them?

INVESTIGATION TIPS

Whom do you believe?

The histories of Gildas and Nennius are very different, but they do agree on some things, such as the Battle of Badon Hill. Gildas wrote that he was born in the year of this battle, whereas Nennius was writing much later. If Arthur existed, can you think of reasons why Gildas does not mention him?

Geoffrey of Monmouth

A key to unlocking the story of Arthur is Geoffrey of Monmouth. Many other writers who have written about the heroic king of the Britons have based their story on what Geoffrey wrote. But can we trust him?

Geoffrey of Monmouth was probably born on the border between England and Wales. In his writings, he names this area as the home of Arthur's castle. Geoffrey wrote the story of Arthur while he was a priest in Oxford in about 1129. If he did make the story up, what was his motive?

TOP SECRET

Geoffrey claimed that the details of Arthur's story came from "a certain very ancient book written in the British language" that only he had access to. That sounds a bit suspicious, but it is possible that Geoffrey had access to a handwritten manuscript that has since been lost.

Geoffrey of Monmouth's book *History of the Kings of Britain* was a best-seller at the time. There were no printed books so copies were written out by hand. More than 200 copies of the book still survive today.

Dangerous times

Geoffrey of Monmouth lived in a time of change and violence. The Normans invaded England in 1066. They had defeated the Anglo-Saxons and would soon crush the resistance in Wales. Geoffrey's book also told a long story of violence and change. It is the story of many British kings over 2,000 years. This story suited the new Norman authorities as it reminded people that the Anglo-Saxons had once been invaders too. He certainly couldn't risk upsetting the Normans. Luckily, his story mixing facts and legends proved very popular.

A love of lying?

Geoffrey was writing about 600 years after Arthur died. Does this make Geoffrey a convincing witness? William of Newburgh wrote his own history of Britain soon after, in the 1190s, and was not a fan of Geoffrey. He said Geoffrey made things up "either from an inordinate love of lying or for the sake of pleasing the British".

Geoffrey would not have risked upsetting the Normans, who ruled from imposing castles such as the Tower of London.

The legend of the Holy Grail

If the events in Geoffrey of Monmouth's writings are difficult to prove true, the story gets even murkier after that. Geoffrey wrote in Latin, a language that was spoken and read by educated people in many parts of Europe. Most ordinary people were not educated and could not read at all. Because of this, many tales were told through oral storytelling. People across Europe started to tell their own versions of the legend. The stories were particularly popular in the French-speaking lands ruled by Henry II, King of England from 1154 to 1189.

French writer Chrétien de Troyes first linked Arthur with the Holy Grail in a poem written around 1180. In the story, one of Arthur's knights is travelling through a ruined land when he sees the Grail, or cup. In later versions, the tale of Arthur is more about the quest for the Holy Grail than the battle against the Anglo-Saxons. Other versions say the Grail is actually a plate.

The Holy Grail was a relic from the life of Jesus Christ.

Knights and magicians

Medieval writers also added new ingredients to the legend. For example, all members of the Knights of the Round Table were said to be equal. Also, Merlin the magician was introduced as Arthur's adviser. Stories were even written about individual knights, such as the poem *Sir Gawain and the Green Knight*.

TOP SECRET

In medieval times, there were actually fights between those who believed Arthur existed and those who didn't. There are stories of travellers being attacked for saying that the stories were not true.

Medieval writers often set part of their tales of Arthur in France, including locations such as Mont St Michel.

INVESTIGATION TIPS

Stick to the topic

Some of the details added in medieval times were based on real people and places. However, these details can confuse the picture, making it more difficult for us to find out the truth.

ON THE TRAIL OF ARTHUR

We could read the stories about Arthur and try to guess which ones are true, but this won't give us any hard evidence. We'll only uncover the secrets of the places linked to Arthur's life by exploring the objects and remains left behind there. A good place to start is the king's supposed birthplace in Tintagel, Cornwall.

Tintagel Castle clings to the rocks of the north Cornwall coast, in southwest England. It was used as a fortress from Roman times. Archaeologists have found the remains of buildings from the Dark Ages, built before 700 CE. This means it could have been a home for Arthur. The area was used by the rulers of Devon and Cornwall, but could it also have been home to Arthur himself? Tintagel was abandoned for around 500 years after about 700 CE. A castle was built there around 1233, but this was too late for King Arthur to have lived there.

Some people still link the castle with the legend of Arthur. However, no one can be sure why Geoffrey of Monmouth picked it as Arthur's birthplace. He may have known something that the physical remains of stones and buildings cannot reveal.

At the time when Geoffrey of Monmouth wrote about Tintagel, it was the 1100s, and there was no castle on this site. He may have learned about an old castle from a manuscript that was written nearer the time.

THE SCIENCE

Testing ancient remains

Archaeologists have many ways to date the remains they find in the ground. For example, the deeper something is buried, the older it is. They can also study the materials used in broken pottery to find out when and where they were made.

TOP SECRET

In 1998 at Tintagel, archaeologists discovered a stone slab engraved with the word "Artognov" or "Artognou". This could be a Latin variation of Arthur's name, but no one can be certain if there is a link.

The castle at Tintagel was probably built because of the legend about King Arthur's birth.

This map shows some of the most important places in Arthur's story.

SCOTLAND

Hadrian's Wall

Castlesteads: possible site of Battle of Camlann

• Chester

WALES

ENGLAND

Caerleon •

Glastonbury •London

•Tintagel

•Winchester

South Cadbury Castle

ANCIENT SITES

Tintagel is not the only site with possible links to the King of the Britons. Here are some other places worth investigating in your search for Arthur.

Caerleon

Geoffrey of Monmouth described Caerleon as the place where Arthur held an important royal court. Geoffrey does not actually mention the name Camelot.

The Isle of Avalon

The legendary burial place of Arthur is often assumed to be Glastonbury, but we can't really be sure what was meant by the Isle of Avalon. Claims have been made for many islands off western Britain, including Lundy Island, Bardsey Island and Iona.

TOP SECRET

Ancient sites like Stonehenge are often linked with Arthur. However, this amazing structure was already ancient during the Dark Ages. For example, the stone monuments were there from around 2,500 BCE.

Chester's Roman amphitheatre was the largest in Britain.

Wroxeter

The Roman town of Wroxeter on the border of England and Wales could have been the base for a powerful Celtic chieftain. It was occupied for many years after the Romans left Britain. Archaeologists have found signs of a great building in the centre of the town, built in the 5th century. Wroxeter is also close to many hill forts that could have provided refuge for the rebels.

Chester

One of the battles recorded by the writer Nennius was fought at the "City of the Legions", which probably refers to Chester in northwest England. Some historians have even suggested that Arthur's round table was not a table at all but the Roman Amphitheatre at Chester. This would have had enough space for Arthur to address all his warriors.

Silchester

Geoffrey of Monmouth named Silchester as the place where Arthur was crowned king. It was a busy town in Roman times but was abandoned soon after the Anglo-Saxons arrived. Much of the town is still being excavated. Archaeologists might still find crucial evidence to link it to Arthur.

Caerleon

Stonehenge

Glastonbury

THE DISCOVERY OF CAMELOT?

The scene for many of the tales of Arthur and his knights is the stronghold of Camelot. In films and paintings, this is normally shown as a great medieval castle. If archaeologists could find Camelot, they would surely uncover some relic that would link it to Arthur.

The real Arthur's fortress would not have been a great stone castle with towers and battlements. At the start of the Dark Ages, a Celtic chieftain would have based his armies in a hill fort or an abandoned Roman fortress.

THE SCIENCE

Excavating "Camelot"

Archaeologists are sure that the site of South Cadbury was in use around 500 CE. It was one of the biggest fortresses in Britain at the time, with a great hall standing on top of the hill. Pottery has been found from as far away as the Mediterranean. This means South Cadbury was home to an important and well-connected person. However, the evidence linking the fort to Arthur remains stubbornly out of reach.

Camelot discovered?

In the 1500s, John Leland, on the orders of King Henry VIII, set out to find the real location of Camelot. He named it as South Cadbury Castle in Somerset. In modern times, archaeologists have tried to discover if Leland was right. If it was Camelot, this hill fort had already been in use for hundreds of years before Arthur arrived.

Ancient Britain was home to many hill forts that could have provided a refuge for Arthur and his followers. Places as far apart as Cornwall in southwest England and Scotland have been suggested as possible sites for Camelot.

TOP SECRET

Ancient Welsh tales from *The Mabinogion* describe a beautiful white building called Arthur's Hall. Some historians believe this palace could have been near Caerwent in South Wales.

ARTHUR'S BATTLES

Nennius wrote that Arthur fought 12 battles against the Anglo-Saxons. If we can track down when and where these battles actually happened, they might lead us to Arthur.

Historians on the trail of Arthur have tried to find locations for the battles, but they seem to have happened in every corner of Britain. If he was fighting off invaders from the east, wouldn't we expect the battles to be in similar locations?

INVESTIGATION TIPS

Location, location

The 12 battles listed by Nennius seem to have been fought all over the country. Locations included the "Caledonian forest", which was probably in Scotland, to the "City of the Legions", a likely name for the Roman fortress at Chester. Surely Arthur can't really have been at all of the battles, even if he could travel along good Roman roads!

No archaeological evidence of a great battle has been found near Liddington Castle.

Badon Hill

We know that at least one of these battles definitely happened. The Battle of Badon Hill is mentioned in histories from the time. It was fought in either the 490s or around 519, depending on the source you read.

The problem is that we don't know where this battle was fought. Some historians believe that Badon was another name for Bath in southern England. However, the battle could have raged further east around the hill fort now called Liddington Castle, near the village of Baydon. The battle was a great victory for the Britons. If Arthur was leading the troops, his fame would have spread widely.

THE SCIENCE

Arthur at Badon

The Battle of Badon Hill was mentioned by at least three separate histories written independently of each other. *The Annals of Wales* gives us a clear glimpse of Arthur's part in the battle: "The battle of Badon, in which Arthur carried the cross of our Lord Jesus Christ for three days and nights on his shoulders and the Britons were the victors."

What was Arthur like?

Now we have some clues that Arthur was on the field of battle at Badon Hill, can we get a better idea of the kind of man we're looking for? The victor of Badon was probably a rebel leader, fighting a desperate campaign for his country.

Last of the Romans?

The Romans ruled Britain for 400 years. The Celts, who had lived in Britain before the Roman invasion, would have lived alongside the Romans and even married people from the Roman Empire. Even though the Romans had now left Britain, many British families would still have followed the Roman way of life, which only disappeared over a long time. Arthur the warlord may well have come from one of these Romano-British families.

The Celts had lived in Europe since the Bronze Age.

TOP SECRET

Nennius says that Arthur killed 960 men at the Battle of Badon Hill. This sounds like a tall tale. It is more likely that these men were killed by all of his men rather than Arthur alone.

Weapons of war

According to legend, Arthur fought battles with the mighty sword Excalibur. The sword was given to him by the Lady of the Lake. However, we know very little about the battles between the Britons and the Anglo-Saxons because no battlefields have been found. The Britons fought with swords and spears, attacking their enemies on horseback from their hilltop fortresses.

THE SCIENCE

Computer reconstruction

Experts can use real human remains to recreate what people looked like hundreds of years ago. Researchers can scan skulls and other bones to build a detailed computer model of the person they belonged to. This technique has been used to reveal the face of a wealthy Roman man found in South Wales and could also reveal what Arthur's soldiers might have looked like.

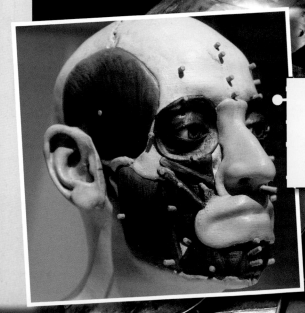

This reconstruction shows the face of King Richard III, whose skeleton was discovered in 2013.

The mystery of MERLIN

Merlin the magician is often pictured at King Arthur's side.

Since the medieval versions of Arthur's story, Merlin the magician or prophet is always by the king's side. We have Geoffrey of Monmouth to thank for the first stories of Merlin. He was an adviser and prophet for Arthur's father, Uther Pendragon. According to Geoffrey, Merlin magically transported the great slabs of Stonehenge from Ireland to Britain. Later, Merlin became a central figure in the legend of Arthur. Could this wizard possibly have been a real person?

Our search for Arthur may have turned up lots of theories, but Merlin can be linked to a real person, or possibly two real people. Myrddin Wyllt, sometimes known as Myrddin the Wild, was a prophet from Welsh legend. Some people thought that Merlin could have been a different Myrddin, a bard who served a chieftain called Gwenddoleu in Cumbria during the 6th century. Unfortunately, that Myrddin can't help us to find Arthur. He was born long after the Battle of Badon Hill so could not have known the warlord who fought in that battle.

TOP SECRET

It was Sir Thomas Malory who portrayed Merlin as Arthur's adviser in his famous version of the story, *The Death of Arthur*. Malory was a knight himself, who turned to a life of crime when England was torn apart by civil war. He was in prison when he wrote the book, which was first printed in 1485.

THE SCIENCE

The druids

Magic was an important part of the Celtic world from which Arthur would have come. Druids were wise men and priests who carried out religious ceremonies and rites before the Roman invasion. The druid tradition may help to explain the stories of Merlin, as the druids were probably still an important part of Celtic communities during Roman times.

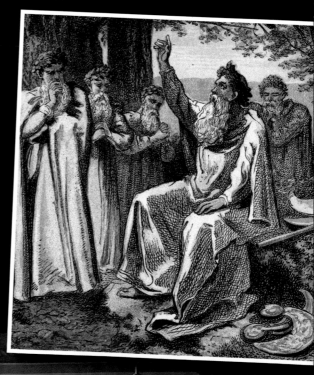

Inventing a myth

So far, we've looked for clues to find out who the real Arthur might be, but what if he didn't exist at all? The main account of Arthur's life was written by Geoffrey of Monmouth. Geoffrey could just have made it all up. If so, why are we still looking for Arthur almost 900 years later?

Politics might explain why the story was written. Geoffrey of Monmouth created a British hero that suited the Norman kings who had overthrown the Anglo-Saxons in 1066. The legends of Arthur showed a time of heroic people and a united Britain – an image the Normans wanted to portray.

Henry VIII seized the treasures of England's monasteries during his reign (1509–1547). We will never know if vital clues about Arthur were lost when the monasteries' priceless libraries were raided.

TOP SECRET

Henry VIII sent out scholar John Leland to discover the truth about Arthur. Leland was one of the first people to study ancient remains as a way to understand Britain's history.

The Tudor quest

In 1485, King Henry VII became king of England and Wales. He was the first Tudor king and had seized power after a bitter civil war. Henry wanted to announce himself as the new rightful British king. He called his eldest son Arthur and the new prince was baptized at Winchester. At the time, this was thought to be the site of Camelot.

Arthur died before he became king. His brother, Henry, took the throne instead. This new king, Henry VIII, was just as big a fan of King Arthur. A large round table at Winchester was believed to be Arthur's original round table. Henry had it painted, with a portrait of himself on it, as if he was King Arthur reborn.

INVESTIGATION TIPS

Why was Henry VIII so keen on Arthur?

The legend of Arthur was very useful for the Tudors. They were able to link themselves with a supposedly glorious time in British history. Henry tended to kill people who disagreed with him, so it was not a good idea for anyone to claim that Arthur had never existed.

Experts have shown that the Winchester Round Table was actually made in 1290 for King Edward I.

GLASTONBURY

The best proof of Arthur's life would be to locate his body. In 1191, a generation after Geoffrey of Monmouth told Arthur's life story, a group of monks tried to do just that. Their secret mission was one of the first archaeological digs in history.

Geoffrey of Monmouth wrote that the wounded Arthur was taken to Avalon, where he died and was buried. A few years later, people began to say that Avalon was Glastonbury. At Glastonbury, there was an ancient monastery built on the site of an even more ancient Roman shrine.

Grave news

In 1191, the monks of Glastonbury began excavating an ancient grave. Five metres (16 feet) below the ground, they found the bodies of a man and a woman, buried with a lead cross. The cross was inscribed: "Here lies buried the renowned King Arthur, with Guinevere his second wife, in the Isle of Avalon."

The ruins of Glastonbury Abbey still attract visitors today.

There were rumours that King Henry II (reigning 1154–1189) had ordered the investigations at Glastonbury before he died. Was the king trying to prove his own link to Arthur by finding his body? Others said that a Welsh bard told the monks where to dig.

In the 12th century, monks were some of the few people who could read and write. These guardians of knowledge could also invent stories if it suited them.

Was the monks' discovery of the lead cross the proof we have been looking for? Sadly, this incredible discovery was not all it seemed. The lead cross has been lost but pictures from the period show that it was probably made around the time of the excavation. We also know that Arthur was probably never called "King Arthur" when he was battling the Anglo-Saxons.

INVESTIGATION TIPS

In the right place, at just the right time

In 1191, Glastonbury Abbey had recently been damaged by fire. Discovering the body of Arthur was a great way to encourage people to donate money for repairs. Was it a coincidence or just good luck or a hoax?

A SCOTTISH ARTHUR

INVESTIGATION TIPS

A man called Artuir

Artuir's story was told in the *Life of St Columba*, which appeared just a few decades after Artuir's death in battle. Artuir was definitely not the victor of Badon Hill, but it is easy to see how his name could be confused with that of another Arthur.

Our search has focused on the Arthur who Nennius recorded. This was the man Nennius said led the British troops at the Battle of Badon Hill, and whose life story was written down, or possibly even invented, by Geoffrey of Monmouth. But there are many other historical figures whose names or actions could make them the true Arthur.

St Columba was an Irish missionary who brought the Christian faith to Scotland.

Artuir mac Aedan was born around 560 CE. He was the son of King Aedan who ruled a Celtic kingdom in the Clyde Valley of western Scotland. Artuir was one of the most feared warlords of his time, although he was killed before he could become king. Some of the battles he fought against the Picts in Scotland seem to fit the battles on Nennius's list.

Hadrian's Wall marked the edge of the Roman Empire. In the Dark Ages it was a great landmark with many fortresses.

The last battle

According to *The Annals of Wales*, the final battle of Arthur was fought at a place called Camlann. Historians believe this could be the fort of Camboglanna on Hadrian's Wall, the border between Scotland and the Roman Empire. It is possible that Artuir mac Aedan fought in that battle, close to his homeland. If so, he is one of many people who may have become the legendary King Arthur.

Making sense of it all

Now you've uncovered the evidence, it's time to make up your own mind. The Mystery Master is looking for answers. What are the most important pieces of evidence that will convince people that Arthur was a real person? Maybe you agree with those people who claim that Arthur is just a legend. Do you think that his whole story has been invented over hundreds of years?

These coins are part of a hoard of 15,000 Roman coins that were discovered in a field in 1992. They were buried to hide them from Anglo-Saxon raiders around the time that Arthur may have been alive. A chance find like this could one day give us proof that Arthur existed.

What do you think of the written evidence?

Many people have written about Arthur over the centuries, but none of them actually knew him. A lot of this case depends on whether we believe Nennius and Geoffrey of Monmouth. Every other story about Arthur was based on their work in some way. It's possible that there were other documents that mentioned Arthur too, but these precious handwritten accounts have been lost.

There are many historical figures like Artuir mac Aedan who lived around this time and may have led armies into battle. One of them could be Arthur or his legend could be about a mix of two or more people.

Can archaeologists help us decide?

Archaeologists have explored some of the most important sites, such as Tintagel Castle and Glastonbury Abbey. So far, nothing has been found that definitely links these sites to Arthur. What evidence could help us to solve this mystery?

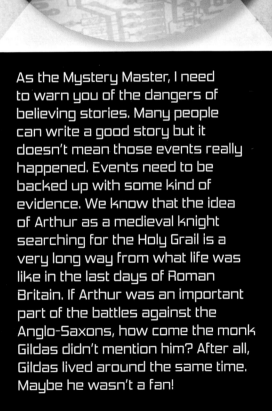

As the Mystery Master, I need to warn you of the dangers of believing stories. Many people can write a good story but it doesn't mean those events really happened. Events need to be backed up with some kind of evidence. We know that the idea of Arthur as a medieval knight searching for the Holy Grail is a very long way from what life was like in the last days of Roman Britain. If Arthur was an important part of the battles against the Anglo-Saxons, how come the monk Gildas didn't mention him? After all, Gildas lived around the same time. Maybe he wasn't a fan!

Will we ever solve this mystery?

The mystery of whether Arthur was a real person has been rumbling on for 1,200 years, since Nennius first mentioned him and his 12 battles. The job of history detectives like you is to unravel the web of legends and stories from the real facts. It's easy to say that all the stories about Arthur are made up. But we may be closer to solving the mystery than ever before.

The discovery of King Richard III's skeleton under a car park enabled us to uncover secrets that had been hidden for hundreds of years.

Answers from the experts?

New scientific techniques enable archaeologists to discover more about the objects they find than was possible in the past. They can pinpoint when historical artefacts were made and where the materials came from.

Using these new techniques, archaeologists have explored many of the sites associated with the legend of Arthur. They have uncovered remains of fortresses and great halls that could have been used by a 5th century chieftain, but nothing that can be linked directly to a leader called Arthur.

Many historians believe that the legend of Arthur is based on a real person, or possibly several different people. Artuir mac Aedan could fit much of the written evidence, but do you think he could have been the same Arthur who led the charge against the Anglo-Saxons at Badon Hill? If not, why?

Archaeologists in 1966 try to find evidence to prove that South Cadbury Castle was Camelot.

INVESTIGATION TIPS

Ask the tough questions

If there's no truth in it, why is this legend still going? First of all, everyone loves a good story, so why spoil it by pointing out that it's not true? This story has also made money for lots of people, from writers and filmmakers to the monks at Glastonbury who claimed to find Arthur's body and received enough donations to rebuild their abbey. Rulers such as King Henry VIII have also helped to keep the story going for their own political reasons.

Just out of reach

Was Arthur the victor of Badon Hill, the king of the Britons or someone else? The only way to solve the mystery once and for all would be the discovery of the true tomb and body of Arthur, or some relic that links him to a particular place. Until then, people will carry on investigating the many people who could possibly be the basis for the legend. The real Arthur may be a combination of more than one person, or he may be nothing more than a legend.

TOP SECRET

Part of Arthur's legend is that he is not dead at all, and that he will come to Britain's aid when the country is in danger. Thomas Malory wrote in *The Death of Arthur,* "I will not say it shall be so; but many men say that there is written on his tomb this verse: 'Here lies Arthur: once and future king'."

Films and modern versions have helped to spread Arthur's legend around the world.

History mysteries

Arthur is not the only person from the past who may be a myth. You could try investigating these controversial historical figures:

HOMER: Greek poet who lived more than 2,500 years ago. There are no accounts of his life, and his epic poems (such as *The Odyssey*) may have been the work of many different authors.

ROBIN HOOD: Legendary outlaw who supposedly robbed the rich to help the poor in medieval England. But did Robin and his Merry Men really exist?

DRACULA: The vampire Count Dracula of Transylvania was invented by author Bram Stoker in the 19th century, but this terrifying figure was based on Vlad III, known as Vlad the Impaler, who was born in 1431.

The legends of Robin Hood and his struggle against the Sheriff of Nottingham probably began to appear in the 1300s.

AMAZONS: A tribe of warrior women first mentioned in the works of Homer. Some experts believe the myth of the Amazons was inspired by real warriors, who may have lived in east Asia.

WILLIAM SHAKESPEARE: Various spellings of the name William Shakespeare appear in official documents – so it's clear this person existed. However, a few people think that the plays of the most famous English writer were actually written by someone else.

TIMELINE

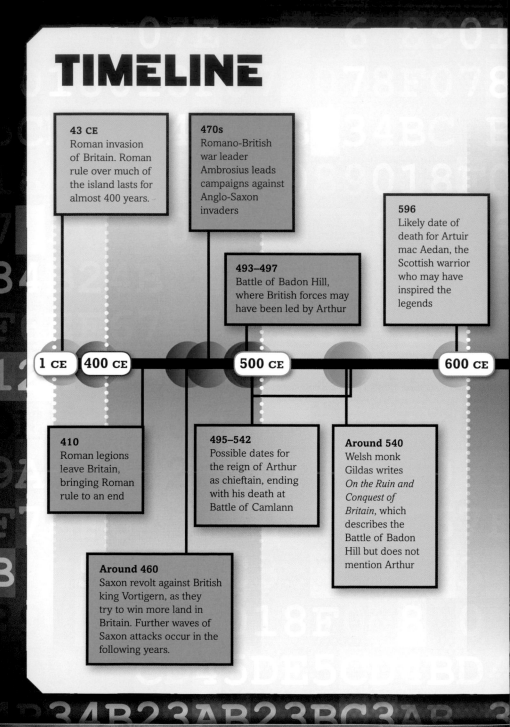

43 CE
Roman invasion of Britain. Roman rule over much of the island lasts for almost 400 years.

470s
Romano-British war leader Ambrosius leads campaigns against Anglo-Saxon invaders

596
Likely date of death for Artuir mac Aedan, the Scottish warrior who may have inspired the legends

493–497
Battle of Badon Hill, where British forces may have been led by Arthur

1 CE   400 CE   500 CE   600 CE

410
Roman legions leave Britain, bringing Roman rule to an end

495–542
Possible dates for the reign of Arthur as chieftain, ending with his death at Battle of Camlann

Around 540
Welsh monk Gildas writes *On the Ruin and Conquest of Britain*, which describes the Battle of Badon Hill but does not mention Arthur

Around 460
Saxon revolt against British king Vortigern, as they try to win more land in Britain. Further waves of Saxon attacks occur in the following years.

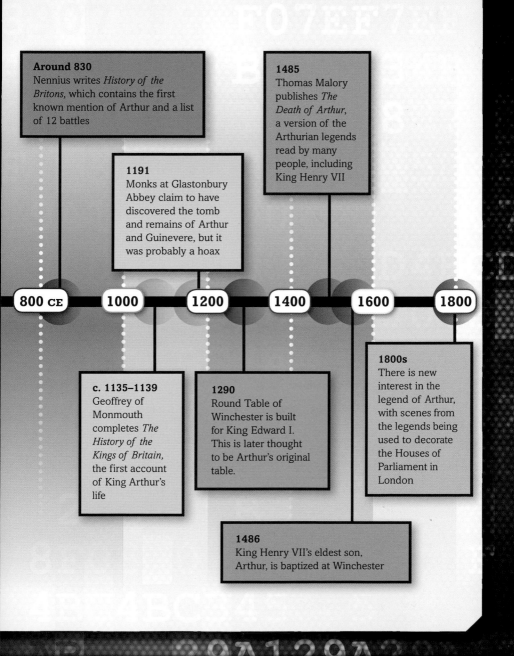

Around 830
Nennius writes *History of the Britons*, which contains the first known mention of Arthur and a list of 12 battles

1485
Thomas Malory publishes *The Death of Arthur*, a version of the Arthurian legends read by many people, including King Henry VII

1191
Monks at Glastonbury Abbey claim to have discovered the tomb and remains of Arthur and Guinevere, but it was probably a hoax

800 CE   1000   1200   1400   1600   1800

c. 1135–1139
Geoffrey of Monmouth completes *The History of the Kings of Britain,* the first account of King Arthur's life

1290
Round Table of Winchester is built for King Edward I. This is later thought to be Arthur's original table.

1800s
There is new interest in the legend of Arthur, with scenes from the legends being used to decorate the Houses of Parliament in London

1486
King Henry VII's eldest son, Arthur, is baptized at Winchester

GLOSSARY

Ancient Rome civilization controlled by an Emperor in Rome, Italy

amphitheatre open-air theatre with seats on rising steps around a stage

Anglo-Saxons peoples who travelled from Northern Europe to settle in Britain after the end of Roman rule, including Angles, Saxons and Jutes

annals historical records which record events that happened year by year

archaeologist someone who tries to understand life in the past by unearthing and studying objects and remains

artefact anything made by humans, usually something historical

bard professional poet, usually employed by a king or chieftain to compose poems and songs

Bronze Age in Britain, the Bronze Age lasted from around 1900 BCE to around 100 BCE

Celts people who lived in Britain before the Roman invasion. Many Celts mixed with the Romans and took on Roman culture, while Celtic culture continued in northern and western parts of Britain.

civil war conflict between two sides in the same country, for example the followers of two rival leaders

court place where a monarch rules with his or her advisers and courtiers

Dark Ages name for the 5 centuries after the end of Roman rule in Britain, from which there are few reliable records

druid ancient Celtic priest or magician

empire group of countries and areas controlled by a single person or group of people in one place

evidence facts or materials that support an idea or argument

eyewitness someone who was present when an event happened

hill fort fortress built on the flat top of a hill, protected by banks and ditches

Holy Grail cup or plate which Jesus Christ is believed to have used at the Last Supper

knight rank given to a king's supporter, often because of his military skill

Latin language spoken by the ancient Romans, and used across much of Europe for hundreds of years

legend traditional story that may be based in historical fact

legion division of the Roman army, including 6,000 soldiers or more

medieval dating from the Middle Ages, which lasted in Europe from about 500 CE to about 1453, depending on the country or kingdom

monastery building that is home to a religious community of monks

motive reason for doing something

Normans people living in Normandy, France, who invaded Britain in 1066

oral storytelling tradition of passing stories and history from generation to generation by telling the stories to an audience

Picts ancient tribes that lived in what is now Scotland

relic ancient object, often with a religious purpose

remains things left behind by people, for example, from previous civilizations

FIND OUT MORE

Are you still looking for answers? You can find more about the legends of King Arthur and people of his time, and the possible real story, in your local library, or by searching online. Here are a few ideas for where to look next.

Books
Amazing Archaeologists (Ultimate Adventurers), Fiona MacDonald (Raintree, 2014)

Celtic Myths and Legends (All About Myths), Fiona MacDonald (Raintree, 2013)

King Arthur and the Knights of the Round Table, Marcia Williams (Walker Books, 2010)

The History Detective Investigates the Celts, Philip Steele (Wayland, 2011)

Websites
There's more evidence out there to explore. Follow these website links to keep on the trail of King Arthur:

www.bbc.co.uk/history/ancient/anglo_saxons/arthur_01.shtml
Historian Michael Wood considers the evidence about Arthur.

channel.nationalgeographic.com/videos/king-arthur
This video from National Geographic looks at whether Arthur was a real person.

www.history.com/topics/middle-ages/videos/dark-ages-barbarians-ii---the-saxons-camelot-begins
This short video from the History Channel explores the legend of the victor of Badon Hill.

When looking at websites, think about who has written the information and whether it is based on real historical evidence such as ancient documents or archaeology.

Exploring further

If you want to dig even deeper, you could explore some of the historic sites that may have links with Arthur:

www.english-heritage.org.uk/visit/places/tintagel-castle
Tintagel Castle, Cornwall: Geoffrey of Monmouth claimed this was Arthur's birthplace and it was probably in use at the time. The castle on this site now was built later than the time of Arthur.

www.glastonburyabbey.com
Glastonbury: The legend of Arthur is closely linked to this ancient town and its abbey.

www.megalithic.co.uk/article.php?sid=277
Hill forts: South Cadbury Castle in Somerset may have been the site of Camelot, but there are many other hill forts that might have been used at the time of Arthur, such as those near the town of Wroxeter.

www.nationaltrust.org.uk/hadrians-wall
Hadrian's Wall: This great fortification can still be seen stretching across Britain. Visit the museums at Housesteads and Vindolanda to discover more about life on the edge of the Roman Empire.

Film and TV

The amazing tales of Arthur and his knights have always been popular subjects for films and TV programmes, such as the BBC TV series *Merlin*. They often use parts of the legend to tell stories of knights and heroism. You may also find documentaries on the subject, such as Michael Wood's *In Search of Myths and Heroes*, which tries to unravel the mystery of the real Arthur.

INDEX